Internal Geography

Books by Richard Harteis

Fourteen Women (1979)
Morocco Journal (1981)
Internal Geography (1987)

INTERNAL GEOGRAPHY

poems by

Richard Harteis

Carnegie Mellon University Press
Pittsburgh 1987

Acknowledgments

Grateful acknowledgment is made to the following in which some of these poems first appeared:

Seneca Review: "Christmas with the Premees" and
  "Work in Progress."
Small Pond: "Pedagogy" and "Mirage."
Three Rivers Poetry Journal: "Genetics."

The publication of this book is supported by grants from the National Endowment for the Arts in Washington, D.C., a Federal agency, and by the Pennsylvania Council on the Arts.

Carnegie Mellon University Press books are distributed by Harper and Row, Publishers.

Library of Congress Catalog Number 86-72301
ISBN 0-88748-038-1
ISBN 0-88748-039-X Pbk.

AGAIN, FOR WILLIAM

Contents

I Frontier of Love

Winter Lesson

There were nights the snow began as powder
dusting the ceramic bulldog on the step
until by morning he wore a white bowler
or was buried altogether. Others,
these gentle fields became moonscape,
a polished crust thick enough to
hold a man without snowshoes. Clear then,
with brittle stars and a freeze so deep
the earth seemed finally irreparable—
you would die if you went too far from home.

Often I lay like a spoiled hibernating bear
after too many nightcaps or excesses
sure the cold would numb me to death, when
the cave grew warmer somehow with dreams of
plump fish hiding in the rainbows of spring streams.

Once I actually woke and stumbled down to
catch you in your father's woolen bathrobe
feeding logs into the wood stove, a dream too.
You could have been counting thousand dollar bills
or preparing the first martini of the day.

Twice a night throughout winter and just before
dawn smashed through the the kitchen and required
breakfast, you danced this ritual. Sometimes I came down
to smoked ham and eggs over light and remembered to
complain how cold I'd been and how your odd movements
wakened me in the night. The heat I accepted like air.

Now I sit in the same woolen robe
wondering how soon the light will come, and
if these logs will hold till then. You,
can't take the stairs as well anymore. Your
circulation's poor. Sometimes you shake a little
in your sleep. I hold you tighter till its over
or I stoke the fire. I know the ritual like a

well-trained dancing bear. More than habit though, sometimes the tenderness I come to as I watch you curl into the warmth of your sleep feels like perfect instinct, like slapping the wet air to hook a rainbow.

Social

We steal down river out of Wiscasset
the ship's low horn grieving through the fog.
An obligatory moose lifts his great head
like a drawbridge, then crashes back
into the black anonymity of the forest.

Someone has pulled the plug here. The tide
line smears the granite boulders
like a foul bathtub. The docks become
little ski slopes into the mud flats below.

Under the secret houses of the rich
blinking now in the morning sun
the local poor climb the walls
left by the tide to collect seaweed.
Maine will ship a hundred million
worms this week in crates of kelp
to the Japanese, perhaps, or Saudis.

It will produce uncountable lobsters
and tourists. Like this one the social
hostess has given up on. No longer chases
around the deck to join bingo,
or judge the costumes. I'm lost to the
solitude of this deck as sure as if
I'd gone overboard with last night's
potato peelings. Left to the seals
which cover the rocks like garden slugs
or flocks of rafting ducks mad
diving for schools of fish. Left, finally
to a noon day ocean where the
horizon has disappeared, ocean gone
full tilt where we could as easily
be a wind chime hanging in the blue air
or a ship painted on the breezy curtains
of a summer cottage. All blue and grey.
No difference in air and water.

Floating isolate in the center.
All perspective lost.
Waiting the large blue whale
bursting the shiny surface in song
in air. My life,
oh, my life.

Star Trek III

The fantasy spaceman
returning from death
greets his captain
gingerly: "Jim?"

Spock's Vulcan father explains
that only time will tell
if the priestess' magic
will bring him totally back.
Instead of "the end"
the film's last frames promise,
"the adventure continues."

I want to cry a little:
I grew up on these heroes—
to be as good as Kirk . . .

But life is a little closer now.
We watch the film together
and I explain the plot
the way one would talk to someone
trapped under ice. My manuals say
I musn't convey anxiety.

I remember the day after
weeks at your beside when
you said my name finally.

You were IN there,
KNEW me.

The same shock the cardiac nurse
felt the year before when she
randomly took the tape from
your sweet eyes and they flew open
as she called your name.

We've been in a few
tight spots lately.

All these months.
My loneliness deepens.
I cry in private
when you forget my name.

Still, you love me clearly,
whoever I am.

The adventure continues.

Song

I

A sentinel stands on the garden wall
camouflaged brown or gray, color
of stone, shrugging her shoulders
to hide the small round head.

She could be a mouse in wings, save
for the gentle, "hey who, who who who"
that stops our lovemaking to sing
of spring or morning or mourning.

II

"Dove," you say, and I hear "love." But
we unwrap ourselves to spy her out,
mousey little pigeon on the wall, oh,
a little pretty perhaps, but singing
with the brilliance of a peacock's colors
as though, had He given her plumage
to match her song, the Creator would
have gone a little overboard.

III

"Morning dove," mother explained
when I was a child, "because she
sings in the morning." And for years
the song was like finding a lucky stone
those mornings in the spring of my life
when my blood rose sweet as a sugar maple's
and a dove sang across the world to me.

This, of course, before time taught me
anything of mourning, before the "hey who,

who who who" asked a question or lamented
a loved one no longer able to sing.
Morning or mourning, it's lovely still
this grey spirit singing with all the beauty
and ambiguity of God's love.

Effort at Speech

"Oh man I love you for my life
you are a friend of mine."
                    Morgana King

Today through the mails the World
comes to our little world, this and
infinite world at the edge of
dream where all is yes and no—
object useful and no useful—
you, me, you—where we meet on the
common ground of ritual and manners
to say as all men do, who we are
what we think.

Our candle blackens the flowers
after dinner, the guest clearly
is still locked in his nightmare
and hopes for a little peace here
on the frontier of love. Memory
is as big as primeval cases,
the saxophone.

You take your dream to bed.
I stay up with mine on the page.
I say, I suppose I'll meet the new
nurse tomorrow, arrange breakfast,
make sure all the doors are locked.
You say, I suppose I'll smile to
this and that and let the particular
pieces of my soul fill this room
and your consciousness until
it's time for death or dessert.

I'm cheered. I'm just at 101 level.
But we all begin a new language somewhere.
It is time for bed and non-verbal
verbalization. Introduction to Living 102.
Sleeping with someone you love.
Sleeping with someone you love.

19

Kermit

Summer after summer while we
spread on the beach, the green frog
spread on the Volvo dashboard
taking in the sun till we came back.

In winter, when our bodies overheated
from working out or making love and
the windshield fogged like a southern
swamp, he leapt to the occasion and
doubled as a washcloth.

He saw so much of the seasons
his plush coat turned from
green to gold to mud to snow.

Only the black glass buttons,
eyes like drops of jelly
kept their brilliance, their
good will against time.

"Gray now," you say, holding
the faded mascot like a beanbag.
"Perfect."

Your own hair lies neat as a
Sunday schoolboy, but silver.
And you smile that smile—spring
breaking through the clouds—
that summer or winter can bring
the blood come rushing to my face.

And the frog glows green
in your hand again.

Storm und Drag

The black boy in black satin
pumps and scarlet shirt waist
can't quite get it right in the
legs either—spread frog fashioned
under his chair, baggy nylons like
a second skin. But the face, ah,
there's a black Helen to launch
a thousand double takes.

Body builders, preppies, dikes
like little whales, as gentle,
and dikes in steel eyes, suits,
and briefcases. The first good
day of summer the gay cafe is as
busy as the buggy stage produced
by turning over a rock after it rains.

Indeed, it could have been
Hollywood's version of *Hurricane Keys*
last night when I found you in a
pool of your own sweet blood
bobbing on the bathroom floor with
the seizure like a Punch and Judy show,
the sky flashing with redundant
bolts of blue lightning. Rain enough
to wash you clean almost as the idiot
driver led you to the ambulance.
How certain he was the two-inch dent
in your forehead meant skull fracture.
He could have been arguing baseball
or the price of beef as the bleeding
star spilled down your face and into
your smile. "All right sir," you said
all night long to every "one more x-ray,"
"This will sting a little," "Now you'll
feel a little pinch." When we got home at
three the streets were still steaming.

We sit like drunks having a little
hair of the dog, conspicuous.
The red bulb of your nose, the dark
glasses, and enough gauze to outfit
Revenge of the Mummy. And this over-
weight Florence Nightingale holding hands
with his Clara Bell beside the flower boxes
bright as little rainbows. The drag queens
think we are ridiculous. We can't get over
the vichyssoise, the black boy's face, how
fresh the world can be after a storm.

Parents

for Matthew Stork

The fire that burned in Joan of Arc
that heroic love as she stood against flames
must well spring from some divine source.
And the grace required to continue in life
when only you survive, say, the accidental
extinction of your family cannot come
from any earthly philosophy.

There is a lesser ground, however,
another kind of good manners or
lucky behavior among human animals
as strong as the social skill of geese
who hang for no perceptible reason
in perfect formation against the autumn sky
or brown bears yawning at the mouths of caves
yawning like worn out children who relent,
finally, at bedtime.

This smaller animal spirit is like
a sweet breath in me these days,
as unaccountable as life. I catch
the child before she falls, my lips
are cool against fevered skin. My
screams become butterflies. Suddenly,
I know how to cook rice.

Something is kicking in, taking over
like a rocket booster or the mating instinct.
I could as easily reverse the process
as rearrange my genes. And here, perhaps,
I am closer. Have they worked in me
these lucky responses as surely as
my cheek structure or green eyes?
Has this little duck learned more
than how to waddle, traipsing after?
Like osmosis, do I live
on their green love
I smile into the mirror.
They smile back.

The Brother

printer is so fast
it virtually thinks for you
as though your soul were a
frantic angel imprisoned
in a computer chip.
Page after page spew forth
as clean as sliced mushrooms.

It would sing your grievance
at high c above z,
assign your tale the
fascination of a soap opera cleric:
will he resist the advances
of the fabulously beautiful wife
of the state's billionaire governor,
will he confess to the Bishop
his hot history of pederasty
while at St. Elmo's School for Boys?
When what there is to tell
is only poor judgment, the inadvertent
cruelty of a sick loved one refusing
the dinner you've cooked, say,
or taking someone's side against you.

My trapped spirit tries to
make sense of a new subplot,
tries to keep it from turning
into terminal cancer of falling
out of love, when you wander
up to my desk to show me a photograph.

The woman is wearing a flowery dress
from the 1930's, is smiling,
is petting a large spaniel.

You smile back at her,
dead all these years,

as though she would at any moment
stop playing with the dog and
go in to cook your favorite supper.

"That's my mother," you say with such pride
there is nothing to do but turn off the machine
and hold you.

Epithalamium in October

You two, one now somehow, or
at the beginning of that road.

Perhaps at the ashram
a silent monk watches
color seeping into
the October foliage and wonders
at the power of love. Or
an ancient Rabbi sips
a martini, designing a
blessing for the friends and
food waiting on the deck.
For the last twenty years
he can hardly bear his
affection for his wife,
these colors, such friends.

We each of us bring our
own baggage to the occasion:
I like the big stranger
who jump-starts your car
on a lonely road tonight
who when he turns has
shoulders huge enough
to hide wings.

Speech Therapy

It is the routine eloquence.
"I don't understand. I work. I study . . ."
and proving your point
are unable to finish.
"But you are improving," I answer,
like saying you're
poor or orphaned
because it is God's will.

"Ok? Ok?—All right," you say,
and smile with enough
hope and trust to make
the angels quit Paradise.

Can I tell you the story
as often as a child will listen?
The wicked witch dies.
The lost prince battles his way
out of his froggy nightmare.
All right. All right.

And every night we open
the sacred book to explain
again that A is the first letter.

And before we come to Z
you will plead with sleepy
foggy petulance, "I don't
understand, I . . ."

Then perhaps we'll pray Our Father.
Our Father bless the sleepy prince.
Flights of angels bid him wake
to sing Your praise, to sing his songs.

And if no song then
teach his heart
a secret, silent lullaby
all right.

August, Connecticut

Mother can't account for the pinheads of light
coursing in slow motion at a thousand oblique
angles as though a tiny star-driven engine had
landed in the living room and was refueling under
the lampshade. She puts her hand into the little
Milky Way and recoils: she has spoiled the invisible
filaments of a hundred baby spiders spinning blindly
after birth in the warm light.

Her heart becomes a hummingbird
but she's as calm as the afternoon she
reached for her golf ball and had to shoo
a rattlesnake from the cup first.
Her partner was impressed: "Ya all
played over death," she called to their
husbands on the next tee.

Well, my Italian housekeeper in tube top and
high-heeled shoes has failed again, though
mother is philosophical: "I wouldn't mind her
soft-porn notion of style if she were only winning
the war on the creatures in this house."

And sure there's been
too much rain and sun this summer.
Even the light has gone
green here on the river,
as though we lived on the
banks of the Amazon. Too many
bugs and too much grass. The woods
so thick and green they're black,
life so out of control here
the far river bank might just
rise like a brontosaurus and
lumber off.

We sit in a cloud of citronella

on the terrace daydreaming of anything
you can imagine: your dear brother's
recent death, the lightning cutting
the sky up river, the ominous
fecundity here.

When I hand you the Campari soda—
ruby, refreshing—your eyes are so
full of love you'd think it was
my blood.

II Border of Memory

Mirage

In Memoriam,
Katharine Meredith Goldenberg

A stand of Queen Anne's Lace
catches the infrequent breeze—
a white sail lifting along the shore
where this year's growth of creatures
sends lazy bubbles to the stagnant surface.

A convoy of dragonflies swarms in,
hovers like a rainbow, and
disappears when a blue snake
glides across the lily pads
into the dark deep roots.

The country pond has reappeared, primeval,
as though the seasons never changed
and time stretched out into an infinity
of lime green light and midday heat.

But your memory sings out against that
illusion like a school bell calling for
the end of summer, like a silent angel
with flaming sword.

Was it only last year
you left the blazing heat
and burst into the cool stone cellar
to share a bucket of raspberries
you had picked at the pond's edge
when in your joy and change of light
missed a step and went all flying
staining the pretty sundress raspberry
gashing the smooth brown knees red
before I moved to help you.

How often did you stand like this in life:
vulnerable, a spoiled gift in hand, and
the dignity of a Pharoah.

I climb the granite steps
into the brilliant light
where you smile again
and the white sundress
glows against your tan shoulders.

The dark berries
are as cool and sweet
as forgiveness.

Christmas with the Premees

I

So much gadgetry and blinking lights
you'd think they make them here; or,
a doll display, each boxed in glass,
for Christmas shoppers.
The premees, the little babies.
Bellies as small and delicate as
coffee-jar seals. Finger tips and ears
all too tiny, but perfect.
Puppy-panting, out of rhythm
with their slow-motion breast strokes.

II

The black nurse is covered
in green—sterile. But she hums
an ancient song behind her mask.
She strokes them, she rocks them:
"Breathe little baby, breathe.
You must wake up now
from your dark dreams.
There is a new star in the heavens.
We are waiting for you."

Beach Song

for Jack and Doris Carlson

I   Decor

You can not tell
where the living room stops
and the ocean begins, here
on the twentieth floor.
Not once have we seen
a resident or another guest
in three days. Has someone
threatened Ft. Lauderdale
with an A bomb? Are there 3000
eighty-five year old women
training binoculars on us
as we sit alone on the beach?
Do we only imagine the silent
hum of secret elevators
as security guards deliver 3000
Chinese take-out dinners?

II   Seizure

Suddenly the star within
your poor brain becomes
a shooting star lost in or
the focus of an electrical storm,
imitating heaven, to wrack your
body into frozen night.

Then, as suddenly as a
thunderstorm is over
you are peaceful, the ocean
at rest, your eyes blue, deep
smiling at me.

III   Grounded

"Now you take care of your baby,"
I caution, meaning the one she's
growing, and not the child she's
swimming out with to toss aboard.
Me and Porky are swimming the boat
against the waves so it doesn't
beach again, careful not to lose
our legs while dad dries spark plugs
and jerry-rigs the battery. Putt putt,
cough cough, when here she comes again.
Where is she coming up with these children?
We toss the new one in, I toss her in after.

Finally, a diagnosis. Out of gas.
The captain giggles, his hands
are bleeding. She hands me a soggy
five dollar bill and an hour later they
chug away into the choppy waves.
How did Porky hold that boat?

She's adjusting her sun hat.
Porky is giving a slow wave of
farewell like the Queen of England
and I, I am the slightly plump
Charleton Heston, I am a tan
Tarzan, waving back like
the Queen of England.

Breakfast

Hungover at the hospital coffee shop
the candystriper waitress is so
delicious looking I understand the
impetus in child pornography:
Her hair is blond.
Her cheeks are pink.
Her lips are classic Cupid.
She is wearing tennis shoes.

My goodwill today is so
pervasive, every face I see
breaks into light. Perhaps today
I will die of love.

I manage my order: "Do you have
any fancy English muffins, like raisin?"

"Heather, ya have any fancy English
muffins like raisin?" She smiles at me,
so close we could kiss.

"Ya want that toasted?"

"Sure, why not?"

China

I   The Great Wall

seen from the moon is merely
a pale scar on the planet's wrinkled surface.
Standing here, however, one can't imagine
that this river of stone coursing over the
mountains could be a man-made thing.

Long enough to twice encircle the earth,
you say, wide and high roadway in the sky.
What could it possibly defend?

I see the mongol sentry at his
lost outpost scan the desolate horizon
mesmerized by the dead landscape until
his limbs grow stiff, hair, fingers
all frozen.

This pointless ghost won't leave me.
You and I pose in leather
against the sky and mountains,
the wall a copper ribbon finally
lost to our vision.

A week is added to a lifetime.
Your smile, your strength, your
shy good manners all these years.
I would take your dear head into
my hands, but then would not know
what to do.

You freeze for the camera, give
a little wave. Soon I'll leave you
to your embassy post, your lonely
intelligence, your secret, heroic
boring life.

The middle kingdom
defended still.

II The Forbidden City

now belongs to the People who
swarm through the emperor's palace
like blue locusts. One boy stands
wide-eyed before the temple gate.
He could as easily be gawking at the
Mona Lisa or lost in the gardens of
Mars. He does not know his dragon
blood, of ancestors so proud the
treasures of Europe sent in tribute
rotted unopened in forgotten warehouses.

He has come from the commune
to deliver this week's harvest
and tour the city in formation
to witness the ancient decadence.
Because there is no refrigeration
he and his comrades have piled
a billion cabbage heads on the
street corners of Beijing. Rotting
cabbage fills the air like an illness,
like the soul of the people.

Newsflash

Boy finds fish dropped by
seagull on Wilson Boulevard.

Parents bring home new baby,
continue to love mongoloid first-born.

Lifeguard admires boy's toy BMW
Boy admires lifeguard's tank suit.

Rhonda Jefferson accused of being
a "big booger" by her brother.

After two and a half hours, Jose Rivera
emerges from his bathroom the
spitting image of Dionne Warwick.

Sofie Greenberg finds the perfect dress
for her daughter's Bat Mitzvah.

Sarah James finds another way of
making her husband think he's young
but decides against face lift.

Mechanic scrapes finger—thinks to
use a little blood like oil to make the part fit.
It fits.

Abidjan

My expense report will read
like *Gone With the Wind*.
Our guide drags us around
by the nose a bit much.
Still, it is the Paris of the west
coast.

The jungle of a five star
hotel lobby is stimulating:
There's a former Excellency,
there's a current one, a
shoe-shine boy, the usual
gold, ivory, perfume, etc.
Booming it seems: will
the price of cocoa hold,
will the tribal system work,
will it come out of the forest
to share with us a little?

Its buildings reach for the
heavy sky, a little like
Hong Kong's, etc. Its ministers
are elegant, eloquent, though
it probably has no more reason
for its snobism than Napoleon
or Joan Crawford, Oppenheimer or me.

Mind you, a few miles into the woods
you musn't drive alone at night
or your heart may be snatched for fishbait,
i.e. the non-metaphorical heart.
And the sage can tell one stories
of fortunes stored in China
to foil an elder sister
to provide for a happy old age.

You powder-keg fuse.
You Atlantic emerald.
This little Marco Polo
is taking himself to bed.

Memphis

I   The oldest of the Pharoah's tombs
the most ancient human thing perhaps
crumbles to a beehive, is nearly lost
to the shifting plain. Time has
taken the edges off, will ultimately
work the pyramid back to sand.

II   There is a certain interest in
the infant art of architecture here
and the various lives
spent over centuries to roll this
little mountain up the Nile. It is
a feat. Like harnessing the
souls of Medieval peasants to manufacture
cathedrals across Europe or the way
local parents sell their children still
to rug factories: the tiny hands
suiting the looms' delicate demands.

III I forget what loneliness I'd thought
to cure with this old ruin. I stand
in a line of trenchcoated tourists
against the improbable rain of a desert
winter waiting to tunnel to the heart
of the tomb. We are as silent as
Auschwitz under the grey sky.
A pack of mongrel pups, small, sand-
colored, scrounge for garbage
chase each other under the buses.
I want it over with.

IV The dead air threatens our lantern
as we descend, but we reach the stone
core finally. The Pharoah-God has
gone it seems, is rotting in a museum
corner somewhere where moonlight never
reaches. Our toothless guide makes much

of the intricate carvings meant to
freeze the pharoah's world into stone
for eternity: here are slaves to sing
him into death and here is Anubis
the dog-headed god who guards the fields
from those who'd rob the grave.
Hippopotomi to hunt and birds forever caught
in flight, lifting in vain from the stone sky
to escape the archer god.

As a little joke, or from spite that
no one has paid his bribe to photograph
these walls, he blows out his lamp.
Our blood runs black a moment, a silly minute
our heart knows it is in danger of being
crushed like a plum by these cold walls.
But he rekindles the lantern and soon
we're fumbling about as we enter the
afternoon sun.

V   In that brilliance I see the sand-colored
sire of the desert dogs who thrive somehow
on these fields. His ears are erect, his eyes
fixed, his upper lip curls the way a man
might snarl when he curses a wrongdoer.

He would rip out my black heart
or return me to the bas relief of the tomb

where I pray,

"Too often I do not
enter your dream Lord.
I sleep, my head upon your chest
uncaring of life or death, content
in my sleep, my service."

I awake to your sleep.
I awake to your sleep.

III   Edge of Consciousness

Genetics

for Audrey Garbisch

Yachts in the harbor
mirror the patterns
of geese in the sky
like an Escher painting.
The air has sharpened
and somewhere brown bears
are beginning to daydream.

Hardly in the autumn
of our lives, we cruise through
the pre-dawn fog camouflaging the
silver Mercedes and confess to each other
over steaming mugs of coffee how we've
come to relish the morning, our joy at
the beginning of the day as predictable
lately as lower back pain after lovemaking.

Are there beads on the double helix,
you wonder, which code for more than
the itch to reproduce yourself
or when to turn your hair grey?

What alarm is warning the heart
to love the light, forgive the darkness?
What coaches the blood to sing its praise
for the surprising gift as we reach the airport,
our farewell kiss a preparation and a covenant.

The Buddha of Sokkuram

"The Compassionate Lord grieved so deeply
over the sufferings of creatures that his
head split into eleven fragments, whereupon
the spiritual father, the Buddha Amitabha
picked up the shards and placed them on his
son's head. Thus, the Bodhisattva's power
to see and relieve suffering was multiplied
eleven times."

I   In Sokkuram the Perfect Buddha
rises like a cone of light within
the mountain cave. The white granite
glows. The statue could at any moment
lift, the Buddha open his eyes and
train his smile on you a moment.
"Why have you come here, brother,
your mind a tree of frantic
small birds. Feel the love in these
stone walls. Free the creatures within you.
Forget now, dear broken friend, forget,
forget, forget.

II   You wake from the honeyed moment,
return with sweet clouds of blue incense
kindled by another pilgrim who is perhaps
as lonely, is perhaps as anxious for
perfection and love as you.

The Buddha's companions are frozen
again into bas reliefs about the shrine.
The Buddha dreams of Paradise.
Tomorrow and below the sun again will set
the East sea aflame where now
there are only tiny freighters
tinkering their way to China. It will do
no good to stay the night
or a lifetime. It will either
rain roses or it will not.
For a moment, I have seen
the perfect Buddha's smile.

III   Sun and clouds and forest
weave a living carpet of light
down the mountain path.
Careful of my footing, and hypnotized
a little by the golden lacework
we nearly collide, this young monk
wearing robes like forest shadow
whose hair and eyes are perfect black,
whose perfect skin and perfect mouth
mirror his perfect master.

We hold each other's gaze,
our dilemma mutual and growing.
In only a moment his blush
a perfect scarlet complication like
blood. But we will not turn away.

Oh Bodhisattva why? Why
this face blooming in front of me?
You who see and relieve our suffering,
in one mountain afternoon why
this play of autumn light
the Buddha's smile
this sacred boy's beauty.

Aphasia

Your face brightens
watching the delivery truck
navigate the tiny
labyrinth of Old San Juan.

It tries another approach,
backs down the street
out of my view. But
the dilemma continues,
reflected in the
glass doors of the café.

From where you sit
I suppose you see the driver
throw up his hands and
curse the horns blowing
behind him. Are they
blowing so angrily at him?

You watch the bemused
pedestrians perhaps, or a
cop who stops flirting
with the sweet brown girl
and wanders over to do his duty.

I can only see
flashes of truck headlights,
a girl's blue blouse, a
policeman waving his arm—
the event only shattered

pieces dropped into the end
of a kaleidoscope.

The tables have turned:
I'm the one who must
piece the shards together,
imagine reality from
broken reflections.
I see the enormity of your
courage and close my eyes.

The Club

The Class of '38 turn up at the club to
show they're still alive and share a toast.
One has brought his latest wife
and seventh child, Adam, age one,
soon enough to be Class of '08,
a politician like his daddy perhaps.
The baby's big voice cries, "me, me,"
over the gentle din, warming up.

Mostly, they're retired these gentlemen.
You'd never know from the bow ties and
corny jokes that they were probably as
wicked as other men in their time.

Now they look out from battered eyes and
see there isn't any other point, wasn't
ever really any other point: Now, one
takes another by the arm and explains why
he's alone this year. "Joan worried about
the cat when the tumor appeared," he says.
"Trained him to come to a silver bell when
it was clear she'd lose her voice box."

Men inside old men, the way a beautiful
animal sometimes seems only to be wearing
an animal costume. And oh,

as they savor their lobster mouse, or
laugh at the child as he steals Mr. Fox
from under the Christmas tree, the joy for me
in these gentlemen's eyes is that what one
might at first take for fear, is only their
helplessness in the face of love.

The Grace of Animals

I

Long before the adult flora of
sex, ambition, and money overgrew
the moral landscape, I recall thinking
I might possibly not be able to believe
in a God who denied a place in heaven
for animals, in particular my blue terrier
who was the single friend of my lonely boyhood.

II

I could see their lesser intelligence, I
was reading about dinosaurs then and Darwin
like other boys, even aspiring to Aquinas.
But I couldn't accept that something so
beautiful, something which responded so
completely to my being would become
dumb earth while, I, my brothers and sisters,
and Sister Marguerite would, would what?
buzz eternal in a perfect inanimate rapture,
paradise, glowing Godhead?

Couldn't there be an antechamber, a
little limbo say, some way for Astra
to live with me after death since
till then she was the only star in my life?
I began to read Egyptian theology which
seemed closer to how things ought to be.

III

The good guest recently, I walked
with my host's child and his dog
while the adults drank
night caps and did dishes:
"Feel her, feel her," he said,
unselfconscious in the delight of

her satin coat, a little afraid the
black lab might knock him down again
going for a squirrel, but determined
with his entire small weight (half the dog's)
and soul to try to train this gentle monster,
who had a pretty good idea how to train this boy.

IV

Ten years ago for mother's birthday I
bought a scottie puppy. With pointed
ears and little skirt it was a cookie
cutter version of Franklin Roosevelt's pet.

The dog lived her quiet secret scottie life
all these years, the black eyes, black coals
at the far end of her face structure, hidden
in the bushy eyebrows—the kind of success
one hopes for in life, giving a good gift.

V

This morning, insomniac and firm,
mother calls from retirement and Florida
to declare I must put the dog to sleep.
The pet has become incontinent, a burden to
relatives, snaps at the children occasionally
and is too much an expense.

This woman is as good as Simone de Beauvoir
or Saint Teressa, no irony is lost on her.
It's what has kept her awake all night I suppose,
this coming to the end and telling me firmly
how to deal with age, and loneliness and death
the way earlier she taught me how to deal with
youth and loneliness and life.

Now mother returns the gift, gives me

the chance to comfort, to say, "no,
I understand, but I think I'll try her here,
see if she can be happy here, no need to
put her to sleep yet. You have made your
decision, don't worry, I accept the responsibility
and it's not a burden."

And it is clearer than ever
how if there is a God
he gives us these creatures
to lead us here and there.

The Amaryllis

pushes its green tongue
through the brown earth
to speak of possibilities.

Outside, the rocks are
blue with winter still,
and squirrels chip away
at the fountain's ice.

Soon the plant will shoot
to an obscene green rod
engorged with water and light,
curving up to a bulbous head that
sways gently to follow the sun.

I know the drill, I
watched it like a mongoose,
celibate, all Lent long last year
until the naked pole erupted slow
motion into crimson flower
proclaiming spring, and vitality
and my loneliness.

Maintenance

I

He changes skin like having
body work done on his antique Merecedes:
pay the fancy surgeon and off with
the basal cell carcinoma.
If the engine and structure hold,
one can afford cosmetics from time to time.

II

But the country boy
brought in for the job
leaving his own dear
55 Frankenstein Chevrolet
to tend the rich man's toy
unnerves him just a little:
"Rust never sleeps, sir.
Did you ever hear that one?"

Divining

for Eva Glaser

After three years of her favorite game
the baby stands like a little crab
pinching her mama's leg until the
baffled mother realizes she at last
is being *tickled back*. And then she's
tickled too by the sweet lesson of
how delicate is the effort
to speak to those we love.

This summer, if statistics hold, I'll
have lived a little more than half my life:
a cancer grows like poison anemone, but
the doctors and I have finally interpreted
my body's exotic flowering. Tomorrow morning
the surgeon goes gardening.

I'm feeling the pinch a little
listening for the wings of doves.

Perhaps they'll only whisper a
warning to live part two
with greater love, easy joy.
Tickle, tickle, tickle.

Stress

My eyelids danced
like summer skies
during an electrical storm.

I watched inside
like a good child
listening to tales of
spilt apple carts in heaven
knowing the house was
soon to split in two.

The sores, the leaden eyes
were not me, were not me.

I was swimming far beyond the reef,
would rest from time to time in the
aquamarine, the gentle swell of ocean
so much like the earth breathing the
temptation was to let her do it for me.

The Businessman Goes to Bed

When it's time for
those ole peepers to open
you'd better *open* them
because you have a
big day tomorrow.

You have to perform
in the World.
You have to keep the glow plug
incandescent, i.e. love,
your source.

You must enjoy yourself,
be the Renaissance Man.

You must answer all your calls
and even make a few more.

Tomorrow again you must
grow cells in the exoskeleton
which thicken you against
slings and arrows and permit
somehow, green life in you
to find a gentle host.

This will definitely not be
a mental health day.

This will be a day in your life
as it is currently.

Let us design a
prayer for bedtime:

That it will all work out somehow, Lord,
a prayer like any man's prayer.

Superstition

This will be the poem
in which a large black
submarine appears
as I drive along the riverbank,
astonishing enough—
a small island
coaxed up the Thames
by three grey ships,
the river where if I were
only sailing the little dory
would lure me closer in
like a puppy pawing a scorpion—
I stop the silver Volvo
and think of whales.

Beyond the secret keening
of whales, beyond your fever
and your hallucinations
as you struggle to live
on this southeastern shore
the black barge moves
out of our September afternoon
up the river a while
quiet, graceful, indulgent,
requiring a poem.

Pedagogy

Kinder than usual these technicians
who offer a blanket against the AC
chilling your bones by the hour
as we sit out the serial blood tests.

How do you train the heart
to such common sense? What are
the lessons which teach a man
to recognize another man?

Once I shouted you away finally
when you handed me your plate.
"Just put it on the counter
if you can't finish." And after
a while you returned somehow
with the food cut into pieces
you could eat. A little help
was all you wanted.

A hundred times on the blackboard then?
"A disabled person is not a disabled *person*."
or, "Everyone's a little disabled, from
time to time a little blind or broken."

Pass me that woolen comforter dearie,
and here's a piece of cake for you
with strawberries sweeter than summer.

After Bedtime in December

This prematurely greying hair
is no longer premature possibly.
Possibly it is time to make a will
and dig in for a long winter.
There may not be snow, there may be
gale force anger directed at you
personally or ice flow draining
into your heart like tears.

When nuts and berries are offered,
slip some into your pockets.
Fatten up. God won't hate you
anymore than raccoons in thick fur
begging a meal, or a glutton
dying of a heart attack.
We do what we can to live.
We do what we can to love.

Serving God and Mammon
in the Great Northwest

for Tyler Bourret

Youngish parents jog with baby
in designer buggy—rack and pinion,
though the course is sufficiently
manicured for bowling or shuffleboard.
Wooden shells line the lake shore
anxious for the downy argonauts
to park their trim little butts.
Golden retrievers stand around
anchoring balloons, sport bright
kerchiefs, idiot smiles, their tails
like metronomes for a Mozart piece.
Indeed, a neighborhood search is on for
Papagaena. "Green body, orange cheeks,"
fliers proclaim from every telephone pole
in case, I suppose, some *other* parrot
lands at the bay window during brunch.

The yuppies of Seattle take their
pleasure on a Sunday morning. Monday,
they'll return to the antique shops and
City Hall, real estate offices and
University. It will be time to service
the BMW, and call the nursing home to
check on mother. Time to ship back the
nephew who filled the house with amplifiers
and guitars and racket, and complained
all summer of their materialism. Time to
worry about that too, and whether another
child is a good idea, if they've found the
right career, if their cholesterol-free diet
will enable them to beat the odds. They know
their love will tarnish or deepen as they jog
toward the grave. They do their best with
daddy's Alzheimer's, they're bright enough to see
the future, what a limited concept arriving is,
and so decide to forgive themselves, the
righteous nephew, the sweet world.

Archeology

40, the winters get longer.
I'll harvest my life
careful to take the yellow dog
I grew from the end-of-summer
puppy three years ago,
someone else's desertion.
Put up the sweet dory
airing it on saw horses like
an indian grave and hope
to varnish in the spring, only
save the structure.

An afternoon's gooseberry jam
sleeps under wax seals, the roots
will have to fend for themselves now.
There's a rumor the sun's tired—
not sure where to flee
this fragment.

Work in Progress

I   Tonight under the moon
    and volcano, guerrillas
    stroll, smoking cigarettes,
    careful of cobras.
    In the air, only ghosts
    and ocean noise.
    Gentle mountain mummies
    wait patiently.

    Farther out, white sharks
    mate, plankton drink
    moonlight
    and turn poisonous.

II   A post-operative patient
    who will live, fumbles
    with the light-switch,
    takes a drink and sleeps.
    Perhaps tomorrow
    she will have visitors,
    perhaps they will
    take out the tubes.

III He stands on the bridge
    filled with booze and possibly
    inappropriate despair.
    In any case, he jumps
    and leaves us with
    appropriate despair:
    we can no longer now
    easily talk with him.

IV   This living business, Lord.
       I do believe we'll all
       get out alive. But in the
       interim how good You are
       to give us drama and,
       often, grace. Accept
       this little prayer.

Carnegie Mellon Poetry

1975
The Living and the Dead, Ann Hayes
In the Face of Descent, T. Alan Broughton

1976
The Week the Dirigible Came, Jay Meek
Full of Lust and Good Usage, Stephen Dunn

1977
How I Escaped from the Labyrinth and Other Poems,
    Philip Dacey
The Lady from the Dark Green Hills, Jim Hall
For Luck: Poems 1962-1977, H. L. Van Brunt
By the Wreckmaster's Cottage, Paula Rankin

1978
New & Selected Poems, James Bertolino
The Sun Fetcher, Michael Dennis Browne
A Circus of Needs, Stephen Dunn
The Crowd Inside, Elizabeth Libbey

1979
Paying Back the Sea, Philip Dow
Swimmer in the Rain, Robert Wallace
Far From Home, T. Alan Broughton
The Room Where Summer Ends, Peter Cooley
No Ordinary World, Mekeel McBride

1980
And the Man Who Was Traveling Never Got Home,
    H. L. Van Brunt
Drawing on the Walls, Jay Meek
The Yellow House on the Corner, Rita Dove
The 8-Step Grapevine, Dara Wier
The Mating Reflex, Jim Hall

1981
A Little Faith, John Skoyles
Augers, Paula Rankin
Walking Home from the Icehouse, Vern Rutsala
Work and Love, Stephen Dunn
The Rote Walker, Mark Jarman
Morocco Journal, Richard Harteis
Songs of a Returning Soul, Elizabeth Libbey

1982
The Granary, Kim R. Stafford
Calling the Dead, C. G. Hanzlicek
Dreams Before Sleep, T. Alan Broughton
Sorting It Out, Anne S. Perlman
Love Is Not a Consolation; It Is a Light, Primus St. John

1983
The Going Under of the Evening Land, Mekeel McBride
Museum, Rita Dove
Air and Salt, Eve Shelnutt
Nightseasons, Peter Cooley

1984
Falling From Stardom, Jonathan Holden
Miracle Mile, Ed Ochester
Girlfriends and Wives, Robert Wallace
Earthly Purposes, Jay Meek
Not Dancing, Stephen Dunn
The Man in the Middle, Gregory Djanikian
A Heart Out of This World, David James
All You Have in Common, Dara Wier

1985
Smoke From the Fires, Michael Dennis Browne
Full of Lust and Good Usage, Stephen Dunn (2nd edition)
Far and Away, Mark Jarman
Anniversary of the Air, Michael Waters

To the House Ghost, Paula Rankin
Midwinter Transport, Anne Bromley

1986
Seals in the Inner Harbor, Brendan Galvin
Thomas and Beulah, Rita Dove
Further Adventures With You, C. D. Wright
Fifteen to Infinity, Ruth Fainlight
False Statements, Jim Hall
When There Are No Secrets, C. G. Hanzlicek

1987
Some Gangster Pain, Gillian Conoley
Other Children, Lawrence Raab
Internal Geography, Richard Harteis
The Van Gogh Notebook, Peter Cooley
A Circus of Needs, Stephen Dunn (2nd edition)